Fortitude
A Necessary Possession

Fortitude
A Necessary Possession

ROBERT L. MARTIN

FORTITUDE
A Necessary Possession
By Robert L. Martin

Copyright 2017
All rights reserved.

No part of this book may be used or reproduced by any means, graphic, electronic, or mechanical, including photocopying, recording, taping or by any information storage retrieval system without the written permission of the publisher except in the case of brief quotations embodied in critical articles and review.

All Scripture quotations, unless otherwise noted, are taken from the Holy Bible, King James Version (Public Domain).

Scripture quotations marked (NKJV) are taken from the New King James Version®. Copyright © 1982 by Thomas Nelson, Inc. Used by permission. All rights reserved.

Scripture quotations marked (RSV) are taken from the Revised Standard Version of the Bible. Copyright © 1946, 1952, and 1971 the Division of Christian Education of the National Council of the Churches of Christ in the United States of America. Used by permission. All rights reserved.

All Greek and Hebrew translations are taken from the New Strong's Exhaustive Concordance of the Bible, James Strong. Copyright © 1990 by Thomas Nelson Publishers. All Greek and Hebrew words are italicized. Used by permission. All rights reserved.

ISBN: 978-0-9993062-0-8

Cover design and layout by Exodus Design Studios

Printed in the United States of America

Dedication

To the glory of God our Father,
Jesus Christ our Saviour,
and the Holy Spirit our Counselor

It is with humble thanks that I present this work for your glory, Oh Lord Most High. You are the One who deserves all honor and glory for the Wisdom given through these pages.
May all who read this be granted *Fortitude* as they humbly seek your Face. I pray that you would manifest yourself to these beloved children in the precious Name of Jesus Christ.
Amen

Table of Contents

Acknowledgements	i
Introduction	v
Chapter 1 First Things First	1
Chapter 2 Seeking to Obtain	7
Chapter 3 Intimacy: The Path to Fortitude	23
Chapter 4 Faith in Truth: The Power for Fortitude	41
Chapter 5 Fortifying the Heart	65
Chapter 6 The Wisdom for Fortitude	77
Conclusion	89

Acknowledgements

I want to take a moment to share my gratitude with the people who inspired me to write this book.

First, my Lord Jesus – I love you Lord! I could do nothing without you. All that I have and all I am that is good comes from you. The inspiration to write was formed in me by you my Lord and I am so grateful that you ransomed me by your blood. I bless your Holy Name for the privilege to give back what you have given me!

To my beloved Paula – You are my love, my life, my lady, my wife! You are a precious gift from God! It is through you, my love, that I came to know Jesus more intimately. There are no words to describe how precious you are to me! I love you my Sweet! Thanks for encouraging me, praying for me, helping me through every trial. I would never have considered anything like this, nor other things for that matter, if you had not gently nudged me along and willingly walked with me through the difficulties. Thank you my love, for reflecting Jesus!

In memory of my dearest friend and brother who is in the presence of our heavenly Father, Pastor Luis Cuebas – Who inspired me to seek after the Lord! He taught me to love fervently and was truly a holy example of what a shepherd should be. I am so thankful for his love and friendship. I know that one day we will sit down with Jesus and have a glorious reunion.

To my dear friend, Marilia Cuebas – Thank you for your friendship and encouragement through all these years. Thank you for allowing me to spend so much time with your husband, my dear friend and Pastor. You have blessed me more than you will ever know and I am extremely thankful for your love and prayers over my wife and me. May the Lord our God return those blessings upon you a hundred fold!

To our friend, Kerry Krycho – Thank you so much for taking the time to edit the first several drafts of this book. It was a great blessing to me. I realize it was a sacrifice to spend the amount of time you did editing. May God reward you for your gracious gift of love.

To my sister, Sharon Justice – Thanks for encouraging me to write a book. It isn't something I would ever have considered on my own. It was a confirmation to me from God.

There are many other lives that have touched mine, which I want to say thanks to. However, it would take a great number of pages to acknowledge everyone. My prayer is that all those who encouraged me, walked with me, and prayed for me will be blessed as this work goes forth.

In memory of my mother and father, who have been in the presence of our Lord and Saviour for many years – Who lived a life of fortitude through war and many distresses. They taught me to seek for the truth for which, I am forever grateful.

May God bless each person who chooses to enter this journey of faith. May you be encouraged to grow in the love and grace of our heavenly Father through faith in Jesus Christ! As you seek, the Lord will guide and strengthen you. He will give you the desire of your heart and you will obtain *Fortitude*.

Behold, the journey awaits, enter in and receive!

Introduction

I was awakened by the Spirit of the Lord one morning with the following thought: Robert, you are to go <u>*deeper into My Word*</u> because right now you do not have the <u>*Fortitude*</u> to handle what is coming. The urgency of these words stirred my soul. Trials had come and gone and by the grace of our Lord Jesus I was on the other side of them. However, as these words continued to burn within my spirit, I was moved to seek the heart of our heavenly Father for fortitude, though I didn't fully understand what it was.

It is for this reason I have written down the thoughts God has given me as I earnestly sought Him. For, as my Lord Jesus revealed to me, others will struggle with trials yet to come and my children need the fortitude to overcome.

I laid out the work to be done in order to obtain this *Necessary Possession* and through my daily walk I have endeavored to write down my discoveries. My prayer is that all who read this will be given understanding. However, though a great degree of wisdom may be given concerning fortitude as we seek, this cannot take the place of your own personal study of the Word of God. The Holy Spirit is the only Person who is able to guide you into all truth, for He is the Spirit of Truth.

To all who read this; may the Holy Spirit of God guide and direct your heart and may you be given the _Fortitude_ to overcome in <u>THE NAME OF JESUS CHRIST THE SON OF THE LIVING GOD!</u>

Chapter 1
First Things First

The Lord instructed me to seek to understand what fortitude means in depth. He made it known that as I sought His Word regarding this matter, I would find what I was searching for. Our Lord's counsel comes in various ways and when the Father brings this type of word by His Spirit to our hearts, we are not to take offence regarding what we hear. For, the Word of the Lord is both instructive and corrective. On the contrary, we are to discern whether or not the words we are listening to are true or false, as defined by the Living Word of God, which was given under the inspiration of the Holy Spirit.

Consider this for a moment, if you will, our past reveals to us that the flesh never dies out quietly or willingly. For, when correction is given we rarely receive it as good. At times, we deceptively believe it to be condemnation. We want to defend our position or give an opinion on the matter. If we allow offence to enter our hearts because of correction, then the blessing that follows will be lost. Rather, may our hearts grow in the ways of our Lord, knowing His instruction is for life eternal. He will cause us to understand when we lack wisdom, if we come asking for it. Let us then rejoice and bless His Holy Name. Thanks be to our Holy Father in heaven for His gracious care. He will never bring a word to our hearts unless He plans to give us the thing we are lacking!

So, the first thing I was directed to do was to seek to understand the meaning of *Fortitude*. Why? Because, I can't petition something from God if I don't know what it is I am asking for. The Lord wants us to receive answers to prayer. After all, He said: "Ask, and it shall be given you..." (Luke 11:9) The *Merriam Webster Dictionary*[1] provided clarity about this word. It is defined as: "strength of mind that enables a person to encounter danger or bear pain or adversity with courage."

Studying this definition caused me to realize it is by the counsel of the Holy Spirit that I'm able to obtain fortitude or accomplish any task set before me. Contemplating these words, I was reminded of the passage of Scripture found in Romans 12:2. Paul said, "And be not conformed to this world: but be ye transformed by the renewing of your mind, that you may prove what is that good, and acceptable, and perfect, will of God." Thus, confirming to me that fortitude is something tangible which can be acquired.

While attentively meditating upon this definition, the word "strength" occupied my thoughts. I understood strength from a natural perspective as one who spent time in the past lifting weights. Strength can be improved through activity and it can be lost through inactivity. This same principle is a spiritual one as well. Our strength

---

[1] Source: Online *Merriam Webster Dictionary*.

in the Spirit is increased as we exercise ourselves in the Living Word of God, or it can be diminished by our lack of fellowship with our Lord Jesus!

The word "enables", also part of this definition, caused me to reflect still further. As the Holy Spirit directed my thoughts, insight was given that we can be empowered with divine strength to deal with or overcome a difficult situation. This word "enable" is a present tense expression implying action. We are enabled, empowered, by the Holy Spirit with strength to handle the obstacles before us, no matter what they might be. John 15:4,5 gives us clarity about this very thing. Jesus plainly said, "Abide in me, and I in you. As the branch cannot bear fruit of itself, except it abide in the vine; no more can ye, except ye abide in me. I am the vine, ye are the branches: He that abideth in me, and I in him, the same bringeth forth much fruit: for without me ye can do nothing." Strength comes as we abide in our Lord and wait for Him.

The last word in the definition of fortitude which caught my attention was "courage". God often teaches us through His Word to be of good courage. Psalm 27:14 says, "Wait on the LORD: be of good courage, and He shall strengthen thine heart: wait, I say, on the LORD." In Psalm 31:24 we read, "Be of good courage, and He shall strengthen your heart, all ye that hope in the LORD." Through these passages of Scripture, I began to realize that only the LORD God can give the courage we need to handle the difficulties confronting our lives; the courage to run the race of life to the very end with the full assurance of victory, knowing we kept the faith!

Journal Notes

Chapter 2
Seeking to Obtain

I asked the Lord to give me the Spirit of truth and understanding for the purpose of obtaining <u>*fortitude*</u>, realizing that without His Spirit it would be impossible to understand or acquire this necessity. While waiting upon the Lord, He directed me to read the following Scriptures:

- Psalm 119:17–20
- Psalm 119:88–89
- Proverbs 8:1–36
- Philippians 4:8

I read the above mentioned Scriptures several times, seeking earnestly to grasp and perceive what my Lord was saying. While I have meditated upon these Scriptures for years, and felt I had some understanding gleaned from my study, the awareness came that if Scriptures are read without applying wisdom, which only Father God can give, one can actually become ignorant of His Holy Word. It is also a fact that our hearts can become boastful with our perceived knowledge if we fail to seek for wisdom with humility.

The passage of Scripture in Psalm 119:17 motivated me to pause and reflect for a great while. For, David said; "Deal bountifully with thy servant, that I may live, and keep thy word." This has become my prayer as I have grown to understand what our heart's passion should be toward Father God.

Deal bountifully — what a beginning! Isn't it wonderful to know that our Father in heaven wants us to pray to Him, like King David, with such boldness and sincerity?

The Hebrew word for "deal bountifully" is <u>Gamal</u>. It means to reward, to do good, wean, to ripen, recompense, to bestow, and deal bountifully with.

Are we able to observe how this is both corrective as well as pleasurable? It may happen that we are being weaned. If so, some of the things our God is removing might cause discomfort or pain. We may even become angry out of our selfishness because He is choosing to remove a hindrance from our lives. Or, if we are in a position where we have learned to walk in maturity, the blessings, which include corrective instruction, that we receive from His Hand become a delight to us. So then, if we ask for the counsel of our heavenly Father in the Name of Jesus Christ His Son, we can expect to receive His guidance, obtaining the very thing we are seeking. When we begin to understand this, our hearts are assured that the trials which come along this journey of life are allowed by our heavenly Father and are ultimately for our good. We pray for His will to be accomplished in us and He will do that! David asked for the sure mercies of God and His care over him with this one word!

The second word I examined was "servant". A number of years ago I did a study on the bond servant. The Lord revealed to me, through my endeavor, that a bond servant is a servant of love who has bound himself to his master because he loves him. This person doesn't ever want to leave the loving care of his master.

I imagine David's cry to God the Father from the depths of his soul was: deal bountifully with me Father God because I am your servant of love. I have found that you love me without measure and I don't ever want to leave your care. I know that whatever you give will be life to me.

This is why I believe David makes the next statement, "that I might live." He was asking the Lord to deal bountifully by reminding Him that he belongs to Him out of love, in love and through love. He is very courageous in doing this. Likewise, we are granted access to enter into His presence by the blood of the Lamb.

What a wonder that God the Father desires us to come to Him in this fashion, with a confidence, assured that He loves us without question and will answer our cry with an abundance of life. We too can pray as David did, asking the Lord to deal bountifully with us as His servants of love, knowing we belong to Him and He loves us. So, we can petition our heavenly Father for these blessings trusting in His love to give us what is best. We ask for God's bounty toward us in all fullness so we might grow in Him, be strengthened in Him and live in Him!

Now look at, "that I might live." This phrase is joined to the first portion of the verse. Through prayer, David asked the Almighty to reward him with life. The Hebrew word for "life" is <u>Chayah</u>. It is defined as: live, alive, save, quicken. The word that captivated me as I considered this definition was "Quicken or Quickening". I personally believe it is speaking of everything pertaining to true life.

The Hebrew word <u>Chayah</u> is also found in Psalm 119:88, which means to be made alive or to be restored. Let's consider this a moment before continuing with verse 17. It reads: "Quicken me after thy lovingkindness; so shall I keep the testimony of thy mouth." Notice David didn't ask the Lord to be quickened because of his good deeds. He asked God, according to His lovingkindness, to make him alive! His reason for this was so that he could truly keep the Lord's Word. Look how this ties perfectly back to verse 17 again.

David asked in Psalm 119:17 for Father God to reward him with His goodness so that he may be made alive and restored to keep His Word. He realized, as we ought, that if we are to keep the Father's Holy Word, we can only do so by being made alive, quickened. David seemed to understand that he couldn't live unless His loving Father God granted him His Holy Goodness to Live and the purpose for that life was to keep His Father's Word, to honor Him. David understood that as one learns to love as God loves, one learns also to love His Word.

To love the Word of God and keep it is to truly know Him and honor Him. We cannot honor our Lord without a love for His Word and without a love for His Word we will not keep it.

The Holy Scriptures proclaim and make clear to us who God is. Jesus Himself is the incarnation of the written Word of God. He,

Jesus the Son of God, became flesh and dwelt among us. So, the Word of God is alive and is quickened to us by the Holy Spirit whom Jesus sent to us from the Father.

When we love the Word, we also love the Father, the Son and the Holy Spirit. The Holy Spirit is the quickening power of God who makes us alive. He enables us to keep God's Holy Word, to worship, to honor and love Him.

If we recognize our Father's love and care for us as He deals bountifully with us, as servants of love, we will also have a passion to keep the Word of God as David did. The Spirit of the Lord encourages our hearts to remember that everything the Father has done, is doing, or will do, is done with, through, and in His great love for us.

Therefore, when correction comes it is always in love. Correction is a reward from God even as other blessings we receive. When we are taught, which can be through correction, it is with love. So, our prayer to Him should always come from this perspective. My Father God loves me and since He loves me, He will surely answer my earnest petition.

Before we move on to the word "keep", I would like to share with you one of my life awakening experiences. I had the honor of spending some time with a wonderful brother in Christ years ago. One day I asked him to go fishing with me because I wanted to hear more of what was in his heart. When we launched the boat and began fishing, I asked if he would tell me more about his life. My friend said with a boldness and assurance that few possess, "I am a new creation in Christ Jesus, old things have passed away, behold all things are new." I knew he was completely taken by the passage of Scripture found in 2 Corinthians 5:17. God had filled his life because he had come to know the revealed truth of that verse and it was made alive to him. It filled his being.

Likewise, I have come to know the love of Christ who truly saved an old wretch like me. He has come and I am no longer the same. It is true that the Liar comes to try and accuse me. He often says, as he did in the garden so long ago, "hath God said such and such…" Are you really free? Why are you sick? Why are you experiencing these problems? Will God really provide for you? So, you think you are loved after failing like you have? To all of these questions my Holy Father in heaven has given me an answer. The precious Holy Spirit inspired me to speak these words to my enemy; "The blood of Jesus Christ avails and His Holy Word prevails, right now."

So, if I have committed any sin, His Holy blood avails for me now! If there is an accusation that the wicked one brings, the Holy Word of God prevails for me now!

I have questions just as many do. I have walked with an affliction in my body for a number of years. There have been days when the pain from this has almost been unbearable, due to an unknown condition which the doctors have been unable to properly diagnose. At times, I wonder how much more of this I can bear, but then my God graciously brings relief. The medication I'm on only helps in a small way. Yes, if you were wondering, I was once a person who thought that if your faith was strong enough then you would be healed and could move on. As I have experienced this affliction, I realized it is God who chooses how He will heal you and when He will heal you. Because of His own providence, I am allowed to experience what I would not choose so I may glorify Him, in, with and by His Strength. God is my Strength and my Healer! He is my portion forever and My God will finish what He started in me because His Word is true. So, I will wait as Job waited, "…until my change comes." (Job 14:14)

It is impossible to walk this way without The Lord. This is what directs me to say with David; "Deal bountifully with me your servant that I may live and keep your word." I know that I am unable to keep His Holy Word unless He quickens and makes me alive by His Holy Spirit, instructing me through His Holy Word! I am weak in this body of mine. It is certain I would falter in faith every day unless He gently leads me on. It is through His gentle leading that, even now, I am led to look again at the word "keep" found in Psalm 119:17.

The word in Hebrew for "keep" is *Shamar*. By definition, it means to keep, observe, heed, preserve, mark, watch, regard, be a watchman over, or a keeper of the Word. As we reflect carefully upon this word, we can see we are to guard and protect the Word; treasure it up in our memory as a prized possession, to celebrate the Word by devoting time to dwell in Him, Jesus Christ the living Word. See John Chapter one to understand Jesus, the Word made flesh.

David asked God for the power to be a keeper of His Holy Word. How many of us have considered this statement in its true context? If we examine it in light of our modern day culture we might conclude that it means to be a doer of The Word. After all, "to keep" requires action. Though being a doer of The Word sounds appropriate, what does it actually imply? When asked to keep the law, we can conclude we are to abide by the ordinances written, whether they are man's laws or God's.

We are often told by fellow Christians to keep the faith. What does that mean? The Hebrew word "keep" gives us some guidelines. If I learn to watch over the Word of God and treasure it up in my heart, when I am confronted with issues that are contrary to His Holy Word, I will be strengthened to hold fast His Word as a treasured possession.

Would we ever knowingly allow someone to steal a prized possession like a home or a car? Consider something seemingly insignificant as a special seat at your favorite restaurant, or the seat you normally sit in at church. How about that parking spot you wanted? Do we become animated when another person takes that spot? The answer is often yes! It seems we can become quite annoyed if what we are used to, or hoping for, is taken by someone else. Please allow me some liberty here! But, if we defend things of this nature with such vigor and tenacity, how much more should we prize and hold firm the Word of Truth, Jesus Christ Himself?

In the parable of the sower and the seed, Jesus taught that some heard the Word but didn't profit by it. It was either stolen from them because they didn't understand, or difficulties arose and since the seed had no root it died. Or, the seed was choked out by the cares of this world.

The keeper of the Word is the one who hears it, understands, applies what he has heard and it bears fruit. In Hebrew the word for "hear", *Shama,* is closely tied to the word for "keep", *Shamar*. There is only one letter different between them. Without hearing appropriately we can't hope to keep the Word. It is extremely essential that we grasp this. Considering the word *Shama,* we find it means to hear carefully, listen with understanding, perceive and obey.

Obeying sounds similar to keeping. One of the most powerful examples of hearing is found in Deuteronomy 6:4 (RSV). It is the prayer known as the "*Shema*" in Jewish culture. "Hear, O Israel: The LORD our God, the LORD is one. You shall love the LORD your God with all your heart and with all your soul and with all your might." This command ties in with what David asked for in Psalm 119:17. We can't hope to keep the Lord's Word if we are unable to understand it. So, we need to know what is meant by hearing. Then we can apply it to keeping the Word. Thus, in order to obtain both, hearing (ears to hear) and keeping (strength to watch and obey), we must be quickened by the Holy Spirit to do so.

There is a realization here addressing our love and care for God's precious Word. To be honest with myself and everyone else, there are times that I fall short of being diligent to follow these commands, just as we all do. They were given to us by God the Father and revealed to us in the person of Jesus His Holy Son, Who is the living Word. Yet, we are careless at times in our love for Him. If we love Him, we keep His sayings as the Scripture declares. He is gently reproving us, not beating us over the head. I love my Jesus more and more every day and I am thankful for His loving correction. It is a joy to me to know that He loves me so much that He would take time to speak gently to me and say, "My son, are you celebrating My Word today? Is that what I meant by keeping My Word?" He brings little reminders to me each day of the things I am doing well and the areas in which I fall short. He isn't beating me over the head with a stick.

I pray as David did that I would desire the Father's bountiful reward so that I am strengthened and made alive to keep His Holy Word, keeping Jesus close to my heart at all times. I desire to remember and be a guardian, a keeper of the things He has given me regarding His character, His manner (ways), His love, His life, Himself, being a lover of God and a lover of His Word (Jesus Christ)!

David wanted to keep God's Word. He asked to be able to fulfill the _Shema_, loving God with his entire being. The word that David wanted to keep was that which is written. I believe this is summed up in Christ Jesus.

Contemplating my thoughts thus far I was prompted to ask the following questions.

Does this relate to Fortitude and, if so, how?

Let's look back at the definition of Fortitude: "Strength of mind that enables a person to encounter danger or bear pain or adversity with courage."

> ➢ So, how does Psalm 119:17 relate to Fortitude? Fortitude is the need for strength of mind and this passage shows David requesting this strength (the

power to live) to keep God's Word. Natural strength is developed by reason of use. If so, Fortitude can also be developed. Exercising the Word with understanding will develop our strength or Fortitude. This scripture shows us how to exercise ourselves in prayer with understanding. This part of the prayer David brought before God is full of instruction. As our understanding of God increases, our petitions become more bold and precise because we have exercised ourselves in prayer—we become skilled in handling accurately the Word and prayer.

- Is Fortitude really attainable? Yes! First and foremost, God wants us to ask Him for our needs in prayer. This passage is a prayer. So, through instruction, we are learning that the power that enables us to deal with danger, adversity or pain is through and in the Holy Spirit, ("…that I may live and keep Your Word") and God will not withhold His Holy Spirit if we ask for Him.

- What is needed to obtain Fortitude? We need the "Quickening" power of the Holy Spirit to obtain Fortitude. God also tells us to approach Him as our loving Father in an attitude of faith. We come boldly before Him because of His great love, knowing He will not withhold His Spirit from us. He wants us to exercise ourselves in prayer and reading the Word, daily being led by the Holy Spirit. Just as David boldly prayed to God in a spirit of meekness, so we should seek with meekness our heavenly Father's Precious Spirit to guide and strengthen us.

It is apparent by considering what God has revealed to us thus far that fortitude is being addressed in these passages. As we continue, we will review this from time to time so we will not forget the process and the prize. I believe we are being rewarded as we study. Still, there is much more to be discovered.

I have been rehearsing the passage we have been studying over and over in my mind for some time now, finding myself constantly in an attitude of prayer concerning this verse. I believe we need to be very purposeful so we might not overlook any insight that Father God would give us.

A thought came to me regarding this passage that caused me to pause once more. It is the message of intimacy with God the Father, God the Son and God the Holy Spirit. Consider that throughout the entire passage, David was approaching the Almighty with an understanding of intimacy and a right relationship with Him.

We are the Church, the people of God, called the Bride of Christ. Yet, I am persuaded there is a lack of understanding concerning this. We are not sure what a bride is supposed to look like. Our declaration is amen to being His Bride. However, when it comes to the practical aspect of our relationship with Jesus, we are clueless, not understanding clearly how to bring joy to the Father's heart as the Bride of Jesus Christ. Believers, at least those who are mature in Christ, have received instruction by the Holy Spirit to continue on in the faith as King David did.

As I was considering intimacy in prayer, the Holy Spirit directed me to talk with my precious wife about this topic, so that I might understand more clearly a woman's perspective regarding this matter.

I have been married over 37 years to my wonderful wife. She has been there through all my ups and downs, the good and the bad, and has demonstrated to me the Love of Christ more than any person I have known. Through our experiences, I have learned much from beholding her. Yet, I fall short on many occasions in expressing to her the Love of Christ. Considering this, I am required to be diligent to show her the love Jesus has given me, every moment I am blessed with. It is a task that demands my full attention. I love her as I love the Lord! The charge I have is to love with understanding, without thinking of what I may receive in return, as Ephesians 5:25 declares; "Husbands love your wives, even as Christ also Loved The Church, and gave Himself for it." The Church has overlooked much regarding intimacy with God the Father and Christ Jesus our Lord through the Holy Spirit.

I've asked my heavenly Father how intimacy relates to fortitude, which is what He said I needed. The more I diligently considered the lessons before me, the more I understood that without intimacy fortitude cannot be obtained. It is given through communion (fellowship) with Jesus Christ our Lord. So, let's press on!

Journal Notes

Chapter 3

Intimacy: The Path to Fortitude

In the pursuit of Fortitude we must follow the path called _intimacy_. Without _intimacy_ with Christ Jesus we can't obtain this necessary possession. Since fortitude requires strength of mind, it must follow that our minds need to be equipped to bear the thing that tests us. How does this relate to intimacy? Well, Paul stated in Romans 12 that we are to be transformed by the renewing of our minds. Our minds are renewed by the things we meditate upon, as Solomon penned. Proverbs 23:7 (NKJV) says, "For as a man thinks in his heart, so is he..." Paul writes in Philippians 4:8 (NKJV), "Finally my brethren, whatsoever things are true, whatsoever things are honest, whatsoever things are pure, whatsoever things are lovely, whatsoever things are of good report; if there be any virtue, and if there be any praise, think on these things."

The Hebrew for "think" is _Siyach,_ which means to meditate, speak about and commune with. If fortitude is obtained through communion (fellowship) with our Lord Jesus, then intimacy can be understood as true fellowship and communion with someone, in and through love.

The love I speak of here is <u>Agape</u>, which is the highest form of love and is demonstrated through our walk or manner of life. Jesus demonstrated His love for the Father by His walk or manner of life. His only desire was to do the will of His Holy Father who *sent* Him. What He was sent to do wasn't pleasant. When Jesus was brought before Pilate and questioned, He said, "…for this cause I came…to bear witness of the truth." (John 18:37) We can't be a witness to something we haven't seen. Again, in John 8:38, Jesus states, "I speak that which I have seen with my Father…" This is a manifestation of love. Jesus demonstrated the <u>Shema</u> of Deuteronomy 6 loving His Father with all His heart, mind and strength.

As we are enveloped in and embrace the Word of God, we become like-minded and are strengthened with fortitude. How then do we embrace the Word of God? If intimacy is the path to fortitude, how is it obtained? Please read the books of 1st, 2nd, and 3rd John, as they will provide a deeper understanding of intimacy.

What do I mean by embracing the Word of God? To embrace the Word of God means to immerse oneself in Him and to ask for an understanding of His heart. I embrace His Word by purposely asking the Lord what His desire is and in what way I should demonstrate it. This is what Jesus did. He saw the Father doing and asked the Father how He was to do it and obeyed.

What thoughts fill your heart when thinking of intimacy? How do you relate intimacy to Jesus Christ or His Holy Word? How long has it been since you've said, "I love you" to the Lord deeply from your being?

My wife and I discussed our understanding of what is involved in intimacy and the following insights emerged as we shared. They are in no particular order, but each thought caused me to become more aware of how easily we can fall short of our high calling to love as Christ loves.

- ➢ Being fully engaged with one another, being totally attentive, involved and committed to each other in every aspect of our walk.
- ➢ Wholly touching and ministering to one another with no other focus.
- ➢ Speaking encouragement to each other. We may say to our spouse that things will be okay, but we don't leave it there. Since we are required to strengthen each other, we share together in love and grace, the Word of God for the situation we are facing.
- ➢ Giving undivided attention to one another, even if we might be inconvenienced.
- ➢ Being free to share with each other our deepest thoughts, those of joy, sorrow or pain, knowing we can share because we are loved, and since we are loved, there is no ill thought concerning what we are dealing with.

- Filling a place in one another's life that no one else could ever fill! (If Christ Jesus hasn't filled me then I have no room for others, I would only be concerned about myself.)
- Joy in doing and being for each other. True love is evidenced in the daily sharing of our lives as we serve the interests of each other.
- Having and expressing the same thoughts and words at the same time (being like-minded.)
- Caring calls during the day to say "I love you" to each other.
- Pet names for one another (we have been given a new name by our Lord that speaks of who we are to Him).
- Knowing we are praying for each other and that our Father is hearing and responding to our cries.
- Growing together over time (knowing Christ more and more each passing day).
- Knowing we are on each other's heart and that everything we do is for one another.
- Being concerned for each other's wellbeing, both natural and spiritual.
- A look, a touch, a fragrance (knowing our Lord beholds us, touches us and He is pleased with the fragrance of our offerings).

- Being needed (worthwhile), as we are worthwhile to Jesus. He chooses to place the care of others in our hands and empowers us by His Spirit to demonstrate His loving devotion to them.
- Singing a song (our Father sings over us with joy).
- Our love being an everyday, anywhere experience, not just a special occasion thing.

As you read through these points, did you ask yourself a question about each of them? For instance, is your love for Christ Jesus an everyday, anywhere experience? Do you spend time giving Him your undivided attention? Do you have joy in doing and being for Christ Jesus? Does Jesus fill you so that you have room to share His love with others? Do you have His thoughts? Do you purposely give yourself wholly to the Lord and allow Him to speak to you or are you distracted? Are you attentive to Jesus regarding the details of your daily activities?

Please understand, if you are being convicted by these questions, it is just the gentle work of the Holy Spirit speaking to you about how He longs to fellowship with you in truth and love. He isn't condemning you, but as I have mentioned previously, He is bringing His loving correction because He desires that intimate fellowship with you. Remember, His correction is always in love!

As I fellowship with Jesus, in and through His Word, I am renewed by His Spirit in my inner man. Then, His thoughts become my thoughts, His ways become my ways and my communion with Him is full of joy, bringing His peaceable assurance to my heart. I can ask what I will and receive it because I know that what I am asking is what He wills. My heart does not seek after any other thing because I am confident that what He has for me is abundant life, given in and through the love of Christ and our blessed heavenly Father.

Since Jesus desires to have intimate fellowship with me, I also desire to have intimate fellowship with Him. He brings to my attention, as He has regarding fortitude, what I am lacking. He does this again because of His great love for me. If I am willing to listen and be attentive to Him, out of love and devotion, He will instruct me in and through His Word enabling me, by the Holy Spirit, to receive what I am lacking and be strengthened with understanding for the task at hand. Intimacy with God the Father, God the Son and God the Holy Spirit will bring about His peaceable assurance in my heart for whatever I may face. The question presented to us earlier was — if intimacy is the path to fortitude, how do I obtain it? The answer is to seek the Lord with your whole being. The Scriptures declare that if we seek Him with our whole heart we shall find him, Deuteronomy 4:29-31. For, the Lord is a merciful God. He has spoken it and it is so. Our God hasn't changed His mind about loving us. Though, we might at times wonder how He could continue to be so gracious. He is not like men. He never changes and His Word is forever settled in the heavens!

Now let's see how intimacy is intertwined with the next verse we will be seeking to understand in Psalm 119 (NKJV).

Verse 18 says, "Open thou mine eyes that I may behold wondrous things out of thy law." I considered the Hebrew word "open", *Galah*, meaning to uncover, carry away, to reveal or show. David confidently asked the Lord to remove the covering that was upon his eyes. He recognized it to be blindness that was covering his eyes and petitioned God for this darkness to be removed. David realized that fellowship with the Holy God only occurred as he beheld Him and his prayer reflected his intimate desire to see.

If we are honest, we all have a degree of blindness. Paul said, "…we see through a glass darkly…", 1 Corinthians 13:12, speaking of blindness of heart. Now, we know David could see naturally. So, it should be evident that he was speaking to God about his ability to see spiritually. In Ephesians 1:17-18, Paul offers up prayers of thanksgiving to the God and Father of our Lord Jesus Christ requesting that we be given the Spirit of wisdom and revelation in the knowledge of God that the eyes of our understanding would be (continually) enlightened. He was praying that we might see with our spiritual eyes.

There are circumstances in our lives when we feel blind and it looks like there is no end to the trial we are facing. We might think it is God's will that we remain in the dark. However, if we allow the Holy Spirit to bring God's Word to remembrance our vision will not be limited because He said through His Holy Son they would come and abide. If Jesus has come to abide, are we in darkness? How could this be since He is the Light of Life? Even if for a time we are not allowed to understand, it is not our Father's intent that we remain there. He teaches us, "…line upon line, precept upon precept, here a little there a little…" (Isaiah 28:10) We are not capable of handling all that Father God has to show us yet. Though, it is His purpose that Christ Jesus be formed in us completely.

Let me share with you an insight I received many years ago, which has helped me as I have walked through a number of questioning moments in my life. I awakened very early one morning stumbling through the house. Extremely tired and not able to see well, I decided to turn on the light. Please understand it was pitch black at the time. As soon as I flipped that light switch, wow, I was really blinded then. In that moment, I was unable to see a thing and it hurt when I tried to open my eyes. Instantly, I heard my Lord say, "That's how it is with you right now, son." I asked if He could explain what He was trying to teach me. The Lord spoke plainly saying; "If I were to reveal to you right now all that I would like for you to know, or all that you are concerned with, you wouldn't be able to handle it. It would be too much for you and would be harmful." He also said, "Little by little, I will open your eyes to see clearly." I know He is still in the process of opening my eyes as I seek Him for direction.

For a number of years I felt as if I were a race horse in a starting chute, just waiting for the gate to be opened. I wanted to get going, to know everything I could and get things done. Then, my Lord came gently to me and said, "Son, your life is not a sprint. It is an endurance race. You will run the race, but at the pace I have set for you. Otherwise, you will expend all your energies trying to do things in your own strength."

When He gave me these words, I was reminded of the virgins in the Scriptures who were awaiting the return of the bridegroom.

There were ten virgins, but five were foolish. They were unprepared, letting the oil in their lamps run out. When the call went forth of the bridegroom's return in the middle of the night, they asked the wise virgins for some of their oil. They responded, "Not so; lest there be not enough for us and you: but go ye rather to them that sell, and buy for yourselves." (Matthew 25:9) They went into town and purchased oil for their lamps, but it was too late because the bridegroom came while they were gone. So, you see, we can be too busy doing for Christ, in a hurry to accomplish things. We can also be carelessly ignorant, thinking that if God wanted me to know He would just give me the answers, while doing nothing. The result of these examples is blindness. If, on the other hand, I practice intimacy with my Lord, walking in communion with Him through His Word, He will gently lead me. I can ask with assurance for my eyes to be opened and He will open them as I walk with Him.

The next word that stood out to me in Psalm 119:18 was "behold". In Hebrew, it is the word *Nabat*, which means, to look, consider, regard, pay attention to, or show regard to. Have you ever looked at something with wonder and awe? This is how David prayed. He asked the Almighty to open wide his eyes so he could see clearly and keenly the wonderful, marvelous, surpassing and extraordinary Word of God. I believe David asked God to reveal His Person and His Holy splendor through His Word. He desired to go deeper in fellowship with Father God. David didn't want to remain as he was and realized if he didn't continue to seek he would dry up. So, this humble servant was being fervent in his pursuit of God, knowing His loving Father would come and reveal Himself to him.

Now we examine the last word in this verse which is "law". The Hebrew word _Torah_. It is the word God gave to Moses for our direction and instruction so that we might understand Him, His ways, and His manner. We are required to take this deeper, understanding that Jesus Christ is the Living Word, the Person of God, who revealed Himself to man. Jesus revealed who the Father was by showing us, through His intimate relationship with the Father, His Heart to and for man. He fulfilled the law because we were unable and gave us access to the Father by His own blood. He sent us the Holy Spirit from the Father so we could commune with Him face to face. The veil was torn which separated us from our Holy Father. For, we were sanctified to enter into the Holy Place, being made Holy through the blood of Jesus Christ. What we were unable to do, God did through His Son. He made us free! Free, yet bound in love; bound, yet free in love; both bound and free in the fellowship of love.

What a testimony we have of amazing grace. David asked God the Father to open his eyes. We, too, can declare as the old song states, "I was blind but now I see."[2] Seeing, I yet desire to see more clearly. Hearing, I yet desire to hear more attentively. Knowing, I yet desire to know more fully. Loving, yet I am desirous to love more intimately.

We have just begun to see, hear, know and love. The old song now has more clarity and meaning for me. The grace of God is truly amazing and sweet is its sound in my hearing. God did save this old

---

[2] The song _Amazing Grace_, published 1779. Words by English poet and Anglican Clergyman John Newton (1725-1807).

wretch and made me a new creation in Christ Jesus, old things passed away, in Him forever buried. That's the intimate love I speak of. I was blind, and happy for a while to remain in that blindness, until He came and opened my eyes. Now, I will never be the same. He removed from me the rags of my sin and placed a robe of righteousness upon me. Jesus has given me an invitation to dwell in His courts and abide with Him forever. That's His love to me and to you.

Some time ago, my heart was in a place of sorrow because of failures in my life. I wrestled deeply with the sins of my past, desiring to be closer to my Lord, but felt it was impossible. I was already aware of the greatness of His love to me. However, I was dealing with my failures in loving Him intimately, the way I truly desired. I prayed and sought Him about what I was feeling and in His loving grace He spoke to me the following words: "Robert, before I created the worlds I thought intimately about you. I (Father, Son and Holy Spirit) beheld you, spoke of you and decided that at such a time I would bring you forth. I knew you before the creation and prepared for you life abundant. I knew that you would falter, so I prepared strength for you to rise. I knew you would sin, so I sent Jesus, who said He would come and be salvation to you. I knew you would accomplish many things and for them I prepared grace to keep you humble. I knew you would decide to do things on your own, so I prepared mercy to heal your heart. I knew you would desire to fellowship, so I sent to you the Holy Spirit, who would empower you to call on me in spirit and in truth. I knew you would experience grief, so I gave you the Holy Spirit who would comfort you in and through My Word. I knew you would experience affliction, so I prepared for you waters of refreshing. I knew you would hunger, so I prepared a large table with fullness for you. I knew you would thirst, so I prepared for you a flowing fountain. In all your days I have been there calling out your name, lovingly guiding and directing you. You thought at times it was your strength, but I was there holding you up. I marked out your days and put them in My book. And, one day, I will call you home to be where I am so that you will be with Me in My house forever. You belong, Robert. You have always belonged. You are a part of My heavenly Kingdom and your home is almost complete. Soon, I will tell My Son Jesus to go and get His Bride and forever you will be where I am. Until then, we will talk of that day and I ask you to share with others what I have said. My longing is that all My beloved children will know that I beheld them and spoke about them before the worlds were formed. The day is coming soon and we will speak then face to face. So, be of good cheer."

My loving Father has spoken many such words to me throughout my life. His words of assurance have held me up time and time again. I long for that day when I shall ever be with Him. I know that it fast approaches and my prayer is that you will be there too. He is calling and waits for you at the Mercy Seat of Heaven to speak with you of these things.

This is what I have seen as my heavenly Father has opened my eyes. I believe this is what intimacy is all about; having the same heart and mind, the same passion of spirit and being purposeful in everything we do, demonstrating the love we have for our Lord Jesus Christ.

If we lack understanding and are purposed in spirit to love our heavenly Father through His Holy Son, we will seek His face in prayer and His ways concerning every situation. When we seek, He will give us His Spirit to see, to know, to understand and obey. The Word of our God declares to us that if we ask for His Holy Spirit, He will not withhold Him from us (Luke 11:13).

This is how I will seek to know Him more and more as my journey continues; "Give me your Holy Spirit Lord I humbly pray, so that I may keep Your Holy Word and may behold Your wonderful, marvelous, surpassing and extraordinary ways."

I continue to contemplate each day what I am to behold and how I am to behold it. As we covered the word *"behold"* and how it related to the passage in Psalm 119:18, God revealed to us that intimacy and communion are a necessary part of deep love and fellowship. However, to clearly understand the intimacy of fellowship with God the Father, God the Son and God the Holy Spirit we need to obtain a greater insight into the word *"behold"*. In Psalm 119 it is meant, to see attentively. Now let's "see attentively" Philippians 4.

Philippians 4:8 reads, "Finally, brethren, whatsoever things are true, whatsoever things are honest, whatsoever things are just, whatsoever things are pure, whatsoever things are lovely, whatsoever things are of good report; if there be any virtue, and if there be any praise, think on these things."

The word *"think"* in Greek (_Logizomai_) means to think, reckon, account, reason, impute. The implication being, to look at the books like an accounting ledger.

We must go to the beginning of the verse to start our accounting process. The word *"true"* is interpreted as; truly true, truthful, truth, loving the truth and speaking the truth. When justifying our ledger, we must balance back to this word. Being asked to think on these things, we must begin at whatsoever is true (truly true, truthful, truth, loves the truth and speaks the truth). If the thing we are dwelling on and abiding in isn't true, then we reckon it to be a lie, unjustifiable, and balance our book (our life) with the truth instead.

The next word is *"honest"*, and it must be balanced back to what is truly true. We reckon it with our book to determine if it balances with what is true, so that in each instance we will dwell with and in what is true. We do this with each portion of this passage and reckon all with what is truly true. Doing so by the Holy Spirit, we find it will point to God the Father and His blessed Son, without whom there is nothing good. So then, if the things we are dwelling upon are from God the Father and His Holy Son, they will be truly true, truly honest, truly just, truly pure, truly lovely, truly of a good report, truly virtuous and truly full of praise. If it doesn't look like my Lord I will choose to lay it aside and examining my life, I will reckon all things to that which is truly true.

This is how we should approach every Scripture. We see clearly that the Word of God is truly true and begin with that on our balance sheet. Everything else is to be measured by and reckoned with the truth. By faith we receive this and move on, always being diligent to balance everything with that which is truly true.

The need for intimacy in our relationship with God should continue to permeate our thoughts as we seek to understand fortitude. Laying aside our old way of thinking, we can be filled instead with what is truly true. Jesus has come to deliver us completely from the old way of life and that includes our former way of thinking.

Our natural man is incapable of understanding the person of Christ Jesus. The old man always considers himself first and foremost. His attitudes are only governed by his natural desires and ambitions. It is true that God gave us our mind. However, if not brought under the authority of Jesus Christ it will only lead us to pride and self-deception. The mind, in and of itself, is just the thinking apparatus. The soul of a man must be reborn and this happens by faith, not by reason. This isn't blind faith as some suggest; rather, simple faith, faith which comes by correctly hearing the Word of God. As we hear clearly what is truly true, and receive it into our hearts, we are changed.

Growing in fortitude is a process. We are built up into a holy temple unto Christ Jesus, through our intimacy with our Lord. Intimacy is the beginning of this journey toward fortitude and will continue to lead us on to perfection in Christ.

Remember, intimacy with our Lord is not one sided! As our Holy Father speaks, we hear and echo what we have heard, asking for His Holy Wisdom about it, knowing God speaks only what is truly true. Through love for our Lord we keep His sayings, not just the things we thought we heard that make us feel good about ourselves. True love and intimacy serves others first, not oneself. God gave us this example by providing salvation through Jesus and His Holy Word instructs us to do likewise. We are to continue to allow the Holy

Spirit to call us back to this place.

    Too often, we find ourselves distracted. However, this should not cause us to be discouraged. But, we should respond to the gentle work of the Holy Spirit, returning to the simple act of faith in Christ and obedience in love.

    I constantly find myself in need of my Father's gentle reminders and I thank Him for them. He speaks to me so sweetly and firmly. Tenderly Jesus leads me on as my gracious Shepherd. I praise Him for His lovingkindness and gentle, but firm rebukes.

Journal Notes

_____

_____

_____

_____

_____

_____

_____

_____

Chapter 4

Faith in Truth: The Power for Fortitude

I have written much about intimacy, which is greatly lacking within the Body of Christ. It isn't that we don't love one another, rather that God is calling us to a greater love.

While contemplating intimacy, the Holy Spirit spoke to me and said; "What of Faith?" Along with the first question these also came to my spirit; How can you love Me without faith? How can you see truth and understand without faith? How can a person fellowship without faith?

I am certain many of you have the correct answers. However, before answering too quickly, remember the instruction is to behold these things from the view of what is truly true. I have been guilty of responding too quickly in the past. After all, I was certain of the answer! How many of you just answered the previous questions? Let me say, I had to refrain from writing what I considered was appropriate the moment these questions were presented to me.

Without the wisdom and direction of the Holy Spirit, the answers would be wrong though they are scripturally sound. When confronted about my opinions, I may feel the need to defend them. This is something that often distracts us as God's beloved children.

If you belong to Jesus Christ and He is your personal Saviour, then you are part of the family of God, and you have something to offer the whole body, which includes wisdom to answer the questions others may ask. It is certain no one answers with truth but through faith by the Holy Spirit, seeing He is the Spirit of Truth.

I was raised in a strict environment and always felt it necessary to prove myself. We weren't the perfect family. Our family didn't resemble any of the depictions one saw on television at the time. Each sibling struggled to be better than brother or sister, seeking for affirmation of our worth. This same conflict is within the church of Jesus Christ and it is not of our heavenly Father. Many endeavor to prove themselves through ministry while unknowingly destroying a Christian brother or sister in the process. It is normal to want to feel good about what we accomplish. After all, we are running a race and want to be first. People in general desire the acceptance of others and there is nothing wrong with this. However, do we look for acceptance to make us feel at ease concerning our own shortcomings? Do we seek to be elevated rather than building others up? Instead of following our Lord's command to be a servant, are we seeking to be served, taking our ease while others are burdened? Many churches have been destroyed by this wickedness. Certainly, we can't hope to portray the love of Christ Jesus with this behavior. He said this is how people will know that we are His, by our love for one another. Our Lord wants us to realize that we are accepted in the beloved when we come to Him, though it is never at the expense of another precious child!

We could all plead guilty of trying to build our own temples without true regard for the temple of the King in our hearts. There have been moments in each of our lives when we've made choices to live by sight, not by faith. Yes, it is true that many of us are Christians. Yet, we have been guilty of leaving our first love born of faith in Christ Jesus our Lord alone. I believe He is calling us again to return to that first love where our communion was sweet and our hearts were tender before Him. As we do this, we will find ourselves preferring one another over ourselves. Though our old life is lost, the new will be much more blessed and enriched.

Now, let's look at the word "trust" as it relates to faith. We find an example of this in the Old Testament in Judges 9:15. To trust means to hope in, put your confidence in, or find refuge. The Hebrew word used here is _Chacah_ (Khaw-saw).

Another reference is found in Ruth 2:12. In this passage we discover that Ruth found refuge under the shadow of the wings of God. It is the same word used in Judges. It is also in 2 Samuel 22:3, 31. Both instances speak of finding a refuge, a covering, or shelter. They also speak of placing our confidence, or putting our hope in God or some other thing.

We can examine our lives and circumstances surrounding us to determine what we are placing our hope in, through the Holy Spirit and in the light of God's Word. It is essential that we allow the Holy

Spirit to give us revelation. Otherwise, we may come to a faulty conclusion that all is hopeless. The Word of the Lord declares that we should not let our heart be troubled. If such a declaration is made, it is certain this calls us to consider where we are placing our confidence. When circumstances arise, which stir our hearts, we must hear the words of our Lord telling us to be still. He breathes life to us through His Word and, if we receive them, our hearts are calmed before Him. The storm which surrounded us no longer has power. We find that our refuge is in Him and in the words He proclaims over us.

Some would say the storm still arises and its fury remains. Yet, His precious Word conquers all. We can see the end of this storm by the faith that Jesus Christ our Lord has given. It is a certainty that Jesus Christ our Lord ever intercedes for us. His intercession conquers every storm, every trial, every foe. The enemy of our souls cannot be victorious. Yes, we find we are weak, but He is strong and invincible. All will bow before His Throne. Blessed be the Name of the Lord Jesus our Saviour.

Another word similar in meaning for "trust" is the Hebrew word *Batach* (Baw-takh). This word involves confidence. When used, it refers to someone placing reliance or confidence in the might of God, someone, or something.

Everyone has a choice as to where we place our confidence. Each individual can pick themselves up, by the proverbial bootstraps, fighting with their own strength. But, this is futile and will only lead to blindness. We would eventually be destroyed by this foolishness, since we have no strength to save ourselves, even from ourselves. By the way, have you ever attempted to pick yourself up by your bootstraps? If you're on the floor, try as you may to get on your feet in that manner, you'll just be contending with yourself. One might place confidence in friends, yet find this trust shaken because friends can and will fail.

What of our hope then? We would become bitter and cynical at the results of this folly. Trust could be placed in the governments of mankind thinking that the good in man will triumph. Yet, this too, will prove to be folly. For, man's selfish desires will always be to look out for himself.

Put your hope and confidence in the Lord. He will surely save. We can only see this by the Spirit of God. The carnal nature of man is utterly incapable of relying upon Him. The natural man will continually find other ideals in which to place his trust. We put to death the deeds of the flesh, that we may walk in the Spirit and fulfill God's will.

By faith, we understand that He is the sovereign Lord and He rules over all things. The steps that each one takes are ordained by Him. The Almighty alone determines the final outcome of a thing. Those who trust, have confidence in Him, will find He breathes into each day His refreshing Spirit. His precious Spirit brings us abundant life, full, complete, vibrant, and eternal. Lord Jesus, we thank You for your breath of life. Holy Spirit come and breathe in us your life giving breath. Bring glory to our Lord through your divine purpose and decree. May the Lord be blessed forevermore, amen.

A third word for "trust" is the Hebrew word _Aman_ (Aw-man).

The first mention of this word is in Job 4:18. This reference primarily denotes support, such as pillars that support a structure. However, it also refers to confirming, being faithful, upholding and nourishing, which speaks of support through different pictures. Nourishment is a supporting function.

For instance, a tree is supported by its root and receives sustenance from it. Likewise, as we are upheld, we are supported by something other than our own means. Through God's confirming work, we are also supported. In Job 4:18, this word is used to denote supporting strength. The Lord God is the sustaining pillar of our lives. He puts no trust in the ability of man. Since this is the case, we cannot lean upon our own strength, wisdom, or abilities. They will all falter. We can and do lean upon our Lord, the foundation of eternal strength. His pillars are immovable. He is the Cornerstone, the Rock of our salvation and our eternal hope. His Word is steadfast and all creation rests on Him.

The fact that many are unable to see does not negate His truth. One day all will behold Him and affirm this truth. The faithful will behold more clearly the splendor of the promises they received. Oh what joy awaits the ones who endure until the end. This is the prize we strive to obtain.

Paul said it this way, "… that I might win Christ." (Phil. 3:8) The things he deemed worthy of striving for were now refuse and the only prize found worthy to obtain was Jesus Christ our Lord in all His fullness. Paul's longing was "to be found in Him (leaning on, trusting and abiding in)…having the righteousness which is of God by faith (abiding confidence)."

Viewing this simply, we see the Word of God is trust, trust, trust, trust…(eternal). The basis for all He declares is out of His eternal steadfastness. When we look at this one word it continues to grow and expand throughout the whole of Scripture. It cannot be ignored, neglected, or foolishly observed. We hold His Word as the precious treasure by trust. This is only the third reference, yet we find it expands to encompass every matter. Our eyes see only dimly now but then we shall see face to face. How awesome God is!

A fourth word for "trust" is found in Job 8:14. It is the Hebrew word *Mibtach* (Mib-tawkh). Its root is from the word *Batach*. Verse 13 speaks of one who has forgotten God. It refers to this one being a hypocrite (godless, profane), one whose actions do not represent who he truly is. The 14th verse goes on to declare that this person's trust shall be a spider's web (a snare, entangling). This reference speaks of the man placing his confidence and security in things that are carnal. It becomes more evident as we proceed to verse 15, which states; "He shall lean upon his house, but it shall not stand: he shall hold it fast, but it shall not endure."

This individual places his complete trust in things he has built. His refuge, hope, and security are in common things. He has no reliance upon God and in fact, by his very nature, abhors God. His ways are in direct opposition to God and in all his ways he defies the Lord. Embracing the foolish as wise, he confides in those who are like himself. This is the testimony of one that cannot bear fruit. This person will be cut away and everything planted by him will not be established, but will be cast out. We see this in John 15. The Father removes every branch that doesn't produce the precious fruit of life.

This is the end of all that place their trust in the things of this world.

We cannot produce fruit in ourselves. The branch that is separate from God has no life in it. So, the hypocrite acts or pretends to be and is constantly attempting to shore up everything around him, which testify of his character. He supposes all he is building will continue on, and since he is carnally minded, he believes that those who see his efforts will look upon them as truth. Yet, our Father in heaven sees perfectly and makes the final judgment regarding every matter. God knows the ways of men and hidden things are exposed before Him.

May Jesus give us understanding concerning our own hearts. For, it will deceive us if we become hardened to the Word of the Lord. Our hope is to be found in Jesus, clinging to Him alone. We should not attempt to strengthen the walls of our own building. For, these walls are things that ensnare us and must come down through true repentance. We build our fortresses, our temples, and our futures, hoping foolishly they will remain. This web, woven through our own doing is a prison, which wraps itself ever tighter around us until it chokes out everything. Deceptions like this can only be broken through the power of the Holy Spirit. His Word comes in power and might and shatters our buildings, and we must let them fall. As we yield, the Spirit of the Lord comes and breathes over us, cleansing us by the blood of Jesus through His Holy Word. By His effectual work we are grafted into the true vine. The Father dresses us and prunes us. He speaks His Word over us, and through His Word we are cleansed (pruned). The Holy Spirit continually comes with the word of truth and breathes His life in us, producing the fruit of our abiding in Jesus Christ. Once He transforms our lives, we no longer need to prop things up. Our being found in Him will be evident by the fruit His Spirit produces. This is abiding rest (trust, confidence). There is true peace in this reality.

It is impossible to experience the peace of God through our own strength. The one who acts as if he has everything together is constantly working to keep them that way. There is no rest maintaining these structures. The rest we find abiding in Jesus is sweet and there is no longer the need or the desire to prop up this thing or that. What we do experience is the wonder of our Lord, in the midst of all our moments, bringing us abundant life. This is the life that produces fruit eternal. The Father in heaven sets us in the proper place. He gives us exactly what we need, when we need it, pruning us in the fullness of His love. This is God's goodness. His pruning is precise, exact, thorough. We can trust His hand. For, He doesn't take away life, He gives life – abundantly.

Each word we have examined for "trust" brings us back to the same place. Trusting in the might of our hands will never bring forth life. Oh, it might appear all is well and we may even fool those around us. But, the fruit produced will soon testify of our foolishness. We will come to the end of our days and the fruit of our doings will be seen. Only through abiding in Jesus can we be certain of good fruit. The truth is, apart from Jesus there will be no eternal fruit. It will all be tested by fire and only the pure fruit of His Word will remain. Truly trusting in Jesus Christ brings us abiding rest.

Job 13:15 says; "Though he slay me, yet will I trust in him: but I will maintain mine own ways before him." This is a fifth reference for "trust". It is the Hebrew word _Yachal_ (Yaw-chal). It is the first time this word is used for "trust" in Scripture.

Let's look deeper to understand why this word was used and not another. It will give us a clearer understanding of the word and its context. _Yachal_ is a primitive root which means to wait, be patient, hope, (cause to, have, make to) hope, be pained, stay, tarry, trust, wait.

The waiting spoken of is that of expectant longing and desire. The word pained is also used as one of the definitions and this is an aching or longing. It is fervent and fresh even in the midst of tremendous affliction. This fervent desire is complete love of our heavenly Father and through fervency we choose to wait, tarry, stay, and abide in Him.

The Spirit of God enables us to make these statements and stand steadfast in trials which come as tests. Yes, the trials we face are seemingly overwhelming and it looks as if the boat we are in is about to sink. However, God has promised never to leave or forsake us. He tells us to get in the boat and go to the other side. Water is filling the vessel we are in and even with all our efforts we can't bail it out. Bless the Lord, for the boat may fill with water but be of good courage it will not sink. He is holding it up! Through these trials we are strengthened as those planted in the Lord. We learn to behold everything with the understanding they belong to the Lord God alone.

Job 13:16 declares the Lord will be his salvation. This was his assurance. He knew that he would come to the end of his days and see his Vindicator, his Redeemer, his Lord. In his suffering, Job was searching for the reason why. We also go through seasons in which we begin to question our trials. We know that our Redeemer lives and His work is full and complete. Yet, we wrestle with the issues, looking for an answer that might satisfy our natural desire. I have been guilty of this on many occasions. We can place things in the hand of the Lord and expect in faith they will be gloriously changed. At some point though, we begin to realize that God has a different plan. It is in these moments we are called to yield all our questions and hopes to God.

I have looked at my own failures as a son questioning why the Lord would even consider using such a worthless fellow as this. Still, His response to me is; "I am the Lord and I will do as I please." The redemption of our Lord should not be questioned, if we walk with Him. For, to know Him is to know life abundantly. We have been purchased with the highest price. We are ransomed by the precious blood of Jesus Christ. The questions have been answered in Him. The answers are eternally sure. We are His and no enemy can remove us from His hand. The response from our heart by faith is the same as Job. For, we shall stand before the King of Kings and declare with all creation He is the Lord. Yet, even more precious, we shall see Him face to face and bow before our Lord and King casting every crown at His feet. Then we shall hear Him say; "Well done."

But what about right now and the future? There is a quote[3] which states, "With faith there are no questions and without faith there are no answers." I can rehearse all of my failures allowing the

---

[3] Source: Goodreads.com. Quote by Yisroel Meir Ha-Cohen

enemy to rob me of the joy of my salvation and ask my foolish questions. Or, I can say as Job has said, "Though He slays me yet will I trust in Him." (Job 13:15) I wait fervently and expectantly for my Redeemer, longing for my Lord now. It is not necessary to wait until we are called home to be with Him before experiencing His wonder. I haven't arrived in my walk of faith. Yet, I am filled with joy to know, that Jesus is the Author and the Finisher of my faith. He will complete all He has started in me. That is His word of assurance to each of His beloved children and He will never ever fail.

By faith in the Lord I know that all my questions have been answered. I may sorrow, but I will also rejoice in my Redeemer and His work of salvation in me. I will glory in the Cross of Jesus Christ my Lord. I will partake of His words graciously and with great reverence hold them. We as His children spend so much time and energy looking at our faults that we lack time to view His work. The abiding we are to do is that of gazing into His eyes, seeing all He is saying, walking step by step in the Spirit with Him, with our ears next to His lips, hearing His heartbeat. This is my prize, to be completely found in Him. May all other things fade away. For, there is nothing so dear as knowing our Father in heaven, His precious Son and the Holy Spirit. Father open my eyes and anoint them to see all that you are, remove from me everything that would hinder your work. Cleanse me, and fill me completely with your love and power. Your will be done, completed in me, this vessel, this home, this temple. Let your glory be expressed through me as you see fit. May your judgment fall on the enemy that has mocked and laughed at my brokenness. May his destruction be swift and complete, in Jesus'

Name, O Lord my King. Lord, let your rebuke come upon him I pray. Let your angels bring forth his destruction. Let your dominion, power and majesty be seen through all that is done. Amen.

A sixth reference for "trust" is found in Job 35:14. This word is the Hebrew word <u>Chul</u> or <u>Chiyl</u> (Khool or Kheel). It is a very interesting word and the use in this passage of Scripture is unique. This is the first time it has been used to signify "trust", which makes it even more intriguing. It has the following meanings: a primitive root; properly to twist or whirl (in a circular or spiral manner), that is, (specifically) to dance, to writhe in pain (especially of parturition) or fear; figuratively to wait, to pervert, bear, (make to) bring forth, (make to) calve, dance, drive away, fall grievously (with pain), fear, form, great, grieve, (be) grievous, hope, look, make, be in pain, be much (sore) pained, rest, shake, shapen, (be) sorrow (-ful), stay, tarry, travail (with pain), tremble, trust, wait carefully (patiently), be wounded.

Job had a friend who was speaking to him at this time. I use the word friend cautiously here, though the Lord also referred to those speaking to Job as such when He commanded them to repent because of their sin. The Lord turned Job's captivity when he prayed (interceded) for his friends.

This friend was speaking of the judgment of the Lord and that Job could trust in God to judge righteously. I consider what is being said in this verse alone. It seems, though he was attempting to console his friend, he was actually rebuking him. This can be seen in Chapter 42 through the first few verses. God was not pleased with the words they spoke to Job because their words were not upright before Him. The Lord said that they had not spoken of Him the thing that was right as Job had done. Wrath was kindled against Job's friends because of their counsel. This should be a warning to us all. If we are to speak, then our words need to be sent forth by the Holy Spirit. Otherwise, all we are offering are words which do not speak what is truly true of our heavenly Father.

In the smallest of things, are we considering our Father's heart? Is the thing I am thinking of true of Him? Does this represent Him as He alone is? There is no excuse in any matter for misrepresenting our Lord. He has spoken to us clearly and explained Himself thoroughly in Jesus Christ. True, we are going from glory to glory and our knowledge of Him is limited to our walk with Him. Yet, He still reproves when we are in error and He will judge if we continue in them. So, we are still without an excuse because He sent His Holy Spirit to teach us. Our lack of knowledge cannot be used as a reason, since we can choose to come before Him and learn of His ways. Yes, Oh Lord, may all we do reflect you and you alone.

As we continue to contemplate the word "trust" and the power of trust for fortitude, may we hear correctly and represent it appropriately to the glory of our Lord. We consider Job and recognize what he experienced before we can comprehend how this word is used. Do we know the character of God as it pertains to judgment in this passage? Thankfully, we can say, yes. We have been given instruction through this book of the heart of the Lord for Job. He honored Job through testing. The Lord never disregarded his lowly frame. He loved him intimately and with purpose He allowed all that took place. He instructed Job and us, as well, through this trial. Though Job felt distant from God in the midst of his trial, never was he without God's watchful care. We are never out of His loving care either, though, like Job, it may appear to be that way!

A number of years ago, a company I worked for made some significant changes. They were very difficult and affected many in different ways. Some people lost their jobs, others were demoted and I was actually given a more prominent role. I can't say that I soared through it all without a hint of the flesh. In fact, I was a little nervous. When it was all said and done, I was also saddened, angry, and ashamed. I had to repent for not trusting my Lord and for placing value on a career. The statement one individual made during a meeting caused me to realize this would happen again. I began asking myself, what will my testimony be then? Whether I would be terminated or not, I wasn't to place my hope in a vocation.

I lifted this before the Lord. The following are some of the things I placed before Him. Was I given a position because of my great skill? No. Did I have such great knowledge that I would be indispensable? No. Can I control every detail of my life and make every plan come to pass? No. These things could become snares to me, if my thoughts were not under the authority of Jesus Christ my Lord. What caused me to put any stock in this career? Who gave me the position in the first place?

I've come to know, by the grace of God, if I find myself taking even the slightest gasp of breath at a thing, it has become too important to me. If my situation stirs me even the slightest bit, it has become too important. When confronting matters such as these, I must surrender it all to my Father in heaven. The surrender necessary, in that moment, is the joyful laying down of myself knowing my heavenly Father truly loves me. He has proven this to me over and over again. The carnal man is unable to receive this. You see, God used this experience to reveal to me my complacency. When this situation arose He opened my eyes to see exactly what I had become. I thank Jesus my Lord for His mercies. He revealed what was in my heart in order to correct me in His love. Now, there is a choice to make. I study His Word and He gently reminds me of what is required. I must die to my foolish thoughts and He empowers me to walk this out. He alone has ordered my life and has the right to do as He wishes. It shouldn't seem strange when something comes my way that I don't want. If my Lord sends it my way, it is for me and the end of the trial will be for His glory and my life. I am truly thankful for His grace and I repent before my Jesus because nothing is so precious to me as fellowship with Him.

The Holy Spirit prunes us through our circumstances. He brings maturity to us through trials we experience. Trials are a means to strengthen and establish us in faith. Father God prunes us so that we might bring forth more fruit and He is worthy of this fruit. Oh, I thank you my Father for your pruning. I ask for the filling of your Spirit in every moment, my Lord Jesus, and I bless you for your wonderful love.

I have experienced an affliction for several years and in this season the Lord has spoken so gently to me. I could try to analyze, which I tend to do at times, why all this is happening. Or, rest in the truth that it is in His hands and it will end to the glory of my Father.

Some of my brothers and sisters have lovingly let me know they are praying for my healing. What a great joy to see the love of Christ being demonstrated in this way. The word Jesus is bringing to me through this trial builds soberness not somberness. Soberness is an unhurried calm, a temperate spirit (self–control in the Spirit), and an earnestly thoughtful character. Somberness is melancholy, depressed in character of spirit and gloomy.

To reiterate, the answers to all our questions are found in Jesus and what He has spoken. We are to live fully, every day, without becoming anxious in anything. Live moment by moment before Jesus in obedience. The answer is obedience from a heart of love as His servant of love. As we obey, we experience His abiding presence. Life is abundant dwelling in His presence. Our communion with Him is sweet and brings forth strength. The fruit produced by this communion will also be a balm of comfort and encouragement to those we are called to minister to while we walk with our Lord Jesus.

There is another question we should ask ourselves: "What is our Lord Jesus saying?" If we are listening, He is speaking. He has spoken to us of walking by faith toward Him knowing He only declares what is truly true. Our response is to obey the counsel and leading of the Spirit. The outcome will be glory to the Lord. Through obedience we bear fruit, which is the word for "trust" we have been studying. As we obey, we dance and sing for joy arm in arm with our Lord. Walking with Christ in faith, His peace will embrace us in every trial, in every adversity. Through trust His glorious love engulfs us until all we see is Jesus our Lord in His fullness. We experience His abiding presence through our obedient walk as well.

"Oh what fellowship divine, I am His and He is mine. In the

presence of the Lord there is fullness of joy."[4] Blessed Jesus, you are my all in all. I give myself to you. Here in this vessel, find a dwelling place. Here in this vessel, glorify your Name. Truly Lord Jesus, be glorified in me and in your people, amen.

So what of faith? If we have faith, we will be Found Acting In Truths Heard (FAITH)! Do we find ourselves there? I said *if* we have faith. However, I should be saying *because* we have faith. You may not have the gift of faith, but you have faith! How, you ask? God has given to every person a measure of faith, see Romans Chapter 12.

We have been given faith to enable us to approach our Lord. Hebrews 11:6 says, "Without faith it is impossible to please him, for he that cometh to God must believe that he is, and that he is a rewarder of them that diligently seek Him."

Would not our God provide a means to approach Him? The answer to the previous question is a resounding yes. Faith in this truth with and in the Holy Spirit gives us boldness to come to Him and obtain from God the wisdom and power to accomplish every task set before us. Through faith we honor our Lord above all else in our ways, manner and actions. We do everything with all our being honoring our Lord. This is the demonstration of love and passion that hasn't been seen by those who have yet to become sons and daughters.

Whatever we do, whether it is relaxation, entertainment or work, it should be done in such a manner that if one were watching you they would see a beacon of hope. The Scriptures declare that there

---

[4] Source: *In His Presence*, Wanda Phillips, Copyright 1973, New Spring.

are three that abide; faith, hope and love and the greatest of these is love. See 1 Cor. 13:13. The love that is spoken of is true love (_Agape_). Without faith there is a separation from hope and love. Without hope there is a separation from faith and love. Without love, hope and faith cannot abide. I often view things as pictures and when beholding this I see the word "abide". Since I understand that my Lord has come to abide *with* me and *in* me, I also see that the three which abide cannot be separated. They are joined to one another and love is the binding cord.

The love of God is our binding cord and His perfect love casts out fear that causes torment. In and through His love we are filled with faith and hope to face and overcome the obstacles we confront. The faith of God is only found in His truth. Again I will quote a Scripture that is familiar to me, though I pray it is not so familiar that I don't hear and understand it correctly. The passage is found in Romans 10:17: "So then, faith cometh by hearing and hearing by the word of God." Correct or right faith comes by rightly hearing the truth of God's Holy Word. To make this clearer, we are required to seek the counsel of the Holy Spirit to hear, that in hearing we hear and in understanding we understand. We often segment our lives. For example, we have faith to go to church on Sunday, but during the week we are afraid to exhibit our faith. My Dad said these were closet Christians and they were professors not possessors of the Word of God. It is true that many of us in this situation are believers, though our strength in this area of our lives is weak. This is why we need to uphold each other in prayer.

God hears the prayers of His people. Yet, I hear people at times say: "If God were so loving where is He now?" To these I say; you don't understand the heart of the Father. He is not willing that any should perish and He waits patiently for the harvest. He will not pluck the fruit until it is ripe. He waits for those who are yet to come to Him. Yes, this does mean there are trials for many others, but I would rather experience the hardships I go through now than to see someone die without hope because I was impatient. God is longsuffering, patient and gently waits for all His little ones to come to Him. However, our Lord will come and what a moment that will be when we see Him!

The questions posed earlier are answered by the Scripture found in Hebrews 11. We are unable to please God without faith and approaching Him must be in spirit and in truth.

What truth must we have to come to Him? The truth we must possess is believing He is God, the God of truth and He rewards us through faith in Him, coming, as the Scripture declares, believing He is God. It is imperative we realize that this believing is through His Holy Son, Jesus Christ. The witness of God is the Word He gave concerning His Son. Please read 1 John 5 to understand the previous statement more perfectly.

Now we need to ask ourselves how faith in the truth gives us power for Fortitude. We understand by definition that fortitude is strength of mind and/or courage to encounter danger or bear pain or affliction with courage. What's the answer?

This takes us back to Psalm 119:88. Here in this Psalm we find the answer: it is in His quickening through faith in truth which enables us to come to God who then rewards us with His power to stand with courage. In His love we are sheltered as the storms arise. No, this doesn't mean we will be unaffected by what others do. On the contrary, we will experience sorrows, but the Holy Spirit will comfort. We will experience affliction, but He will deliver us. We may experience pain, but our God will come and save. Paraphrasing a Scripture from Luke Chapter 18; When the Lord comes will He find us full of His faith working His works in our daily activities? Will we be Found Acting In Truths Heard (FAITH)? We are all in the ministry if we are His. This ministry is that of daily living. We are called to express love to those we meet, through a smile, an encouraging word, a simple touch or a thank you. By these acts of kindness, our brothers and sisters are refreshed and uplifted. I encourage each of you to take some time and pray that the Holy Spirit will strengthen you for this task.

Journal Notes

_____

_____

_____

_____

_____

Chapter 5
Fortifying the Heart

Let's look at another Scripture, Psalm 27:14. Read the whole Chapter paying particular attention to this last verse. "Wait on the LORD: be of good courage, and He shall strengthen thine heart: Wait, I say, on the LORD."

The first word we see is the word "wait". I had to pause the moment I beheld this word. It is summing up the appropriation of faith and, given we are looking at this now, it has great significance. "Wait on the Lord."

We've been speaking of intimacy and faith. Let's begin with the word "wait" in light of what is truly true. This verb doesn't mean to do nothing. As a matter of fact, it has action associated with it. Waiting on the Lord, (Jehovah) the Almighty, means to wait with expectancy. Remember, this doesn't mean to wait expecting to have what you want, how you want it. It does mean, however, that we can wait with a hope and assurance that our God will come and do what He has promised with regard to life (the fullness of life found in our relationship with Jesus Christ). So, we look for Him with expectancy and hope knowing that He will come and finish what He started.

The next portion of this verse says to "be of good courage." You might ask; how am I to accomplish this in the midst of difficult circumstances? Let's consider some things; when our heavenly Father asks us to be of "good courage", He is not asking us to accomplish an impossible task. I know in my own personal experience that at times things seem impossible, but God reveals His strength through my weakness. He is first asking us to do this based on our relationship with Him. He knows we are not able to do anything in our strength, though some might think they are able. If you have strength, God gave it. If you have anything that is good, God gave it. These things are only understood and received by faith.

Examine the Hebrew for "good courage", <u>Chazaq</u> (Khaw-zak). It has many meanings based on context. In Psalm 27:14 it is: to be encouraged, strengthened or take courage. There is a similar passage in the New Testament spoken by our Lord. "…In the world you shall have tribulation: but be of good cheer; I have overcome the world." (John 16:33) The word cheer doesn't mean to be happy, as some might suppose, because happiness is temporal. The connotation in Greek is exactly the same as the Hebrew, to be comforted and/or be of good courage.

I know I can't make myself courageous. The moment I find myself in a place I don't want to be I realize that God Almighty is the only one who is able to strengthen me. So, when we are asked to be of good courage, we are asked to do so relying on our Lord who loves us and cares for us. Based on this, we can rise to meet the day because He has come to abide and has promised never to leave us or forsake us. His word is true and as Psalm 119:89 states, "Forever, O Lord, thy word is settled in heaven." His Word is forever established and He will never fall short of His Word! He loves us and we can be sure of this. His love is what binds us to Him. This will never change! If we have faltered in a moment, still our Lord will never falter concerning His Word. He will raise us up again by His mighty power to stand once more. We are to immerse ourselves in His Word, for in Him we will find strength, but apart from our loving Saviour we will only find ourselves impotent. Our Lord will continue to reveal Himself to us as we seek to know Him in spirit and in truth.

If we need to know how He will give us courage, let's look a bit further into this passage of Scripture. When we contemplate what it means to be of "good courage", we go back to the first part of the verse which encourages us to wait on the Lord. We must remember what waiting is before we move to the next part of the phrase. The next segment says, "and He shall strengthen thy heart." Look at the word "and". It is similar to a mathematical term which means you must add it to the previous term, in this case, "be of good courage." Through this insight, we understand the Lord is the One who will cause us to be strengthened. The significance of this Scripture points back to what we have examined relating to fortitude. The Hebrew word for "strengthen" is _Amats_ (Aw-mats). It means to be made strong, courageous, established, increased and _fortified_! I was so blessed as I was led to read this knowing how wonderful our Lord is to guide us in His truth.

We comprehend from this passage of Scripture that we are

fortified as we wait on the Lord in spirit and truth by, in and through faith, hope and love.

The thread woven through the fabric of this writing is fellowship. The communion of love with faith and hope produces fellowship with God and with one another. The Holy Spirit is the person who empowers us to live this out. He comes to reveal the truth to our hearts and strengthens us to walk in love.

We live in an age that is fast paced, expecting things to be easily accomplished and to have them now. This lifestyle has also become part of our Christian walk. I have been guilty at times of allowing myself to be lax concerning my relationship with Christ Jesus and others because of this very attitude. Many strive for the American dream. Yet, in this season of life we see our hopes, dreams, ambitions being shaken. The hope to retire or just live out our older years in peace is being destroyed because of the greed and foolishness of wicked people. Men's hearts are beginning to fail because of the turmoil surrounding us. We see wars, famine, hurricanes, earthquakes and many other disasters surrounding us and our faith is being tested. What are we to do?

We are instructed by our Lord Jesus to take courage and not worry about tomorrow. The need to be fortitude is great and is only obtained through the precious communion we have with our Lord. Communion through love is never hurried. This fellowship is established by waiting on Him. It is a change of lifestyle, a change in our way of thinking, but it can't be done through will power. The Holy Spirit is the Person who forms in us this attitude. Whether we are working or playing, our fellowship with Jesus should be foremost in our lives. The world is clamoring for our attention, constantly telling us that this or that has to be done now. These voices are bombarding our minds and it seems we are driven to satisfy these demands. There are many voices indeed, but only one voice of truth.

I am reminded of a little boy I knew who would often say he needs this or that and he always stretched out the "e" to emphasize how important it was. Most of us are like this little child. We seek God for what we want and emphasize to Him the importance of our requests. Yet, He tells us that He is already aware of what we "neeeeed" and we are to seek His kingdom first. This causes me again to realize the necessity of waiting on the Lord. The strength we need is given as we enter into fellowship with him. The Holy Spirit gives us wisdom through our communion and instruction for the daily tasks before us. Yes, this means He will direct at work or play. The question is, are we willing to submit ourselves to Him and allow His work to be done through us as we walk out each day?

The Holy Spirit isn't in a hurry to speak to us and move on. The fellowship we have is to be a continuous flowing fountain of prayer. In each moment of the day, we need His divine wisdom, including all the things we know how to do. This is something that distracts us in our walk with Christ. We think we know how to do it, or we know what that means, or we understand what a person is saying. As an example: "I have been doing such and such for a long time; so, don't tell me how to do it." However, we are to approach everything in and with the Holy Spirit. In this manner, we will find a greater understanding of what it is we are to do or greater wisdom concerning the things we have already learned.

Much of how we function is driven by self-perception in each of the circumstances we face. How do we perceive ourselves? Considering who we are in God is important to affirming us in the faith. Feelings are important, but we are not to be moved by our emotions. Yet, many of us have experienced the moving of the Holy Spirit in such a manner that our very being was greatly moved and we expressed our feelings either through laughter, tears or joyful praise.

The Scripture found in Philippians 4:1 is one of many that speaks of who God says we are. We are beloved! Paul speaks to the Philippians saying, "Therefore, my dearly beloved and longed for, my joy and my crown so stand fast in the Lord, my dearly beloved." It is the word that Father God used to declare His love for Jesus. He said, "…This is my beloved Son, in whom I am well pleased." (Mt. 3:17) Here is just one passage that uses this interpretation for "beloved". The word beloved in the Greek is <u>Agapetos</u>. It means dearly beloved, well beloved, beloved, esteemed, favorite and worthy of love.

The disciples of our Lord used this term of endearment to declare their love for the brethren. Brethren; meaning both male and female. We are favored of God and worthy of love. What a statement for us to grasp! This is not something we can understand by emotion or even by natural reason. All have walked through experiences that caused us to feel unworthy, unlovable and useless before God or others, for that matter. Many of us, who have come to a saving knowledge of God, still reason within ourselves that we are unworthy or can no longer be used of God because of past failures.

However, we are to move on from this place and receive with joy His Word of love and forgiveness, beholding what is truly true.

The word _Agapetos_ is derived from _Agape,_ the highest form of love we possess and exhibit to each other. It is the love of God in our hearts demonstrated. Some have used the word love without a clear understanding of its meaning. However, in this season, may we clearly reveal and affirm this love.

Recently, I have noticed myself using the word "beloved". I call my brothers and sisters in Christ Jesus my beloved friends. This is a work of the Spirit of God. He begins to move in us and as He works we are to be attentive to every detail. I believe a more excellent way of looking at this is to be sober and vigilant. Often, I have experienced the honor of speaking to someone and graciously the Lord comforts and encourages the individual when I had no idea of what they were in need of. However, if I were more attentive, then I would also be strengthened since the Word of God is profitable for me as well.

I must acknowledge, it was years of living before I realized how much I was loved and worthy of love by my Lord and others. Past failures were the reasons I felt unloved or unworthy. When I examined my life, I could find no reason why others would love me, let alone God. How tragic for us to go through life with burdens so heavy that we can't see how much we are loved.

We often perpetuate ill treatment from members within the Body of Christ because we hide ourselves and think no one cares. There has been much immaturity in the church because of this issue.

Mature brothers and sisters in Christ should be more attentive to address things they see by the Spirit. However, we often think within ourselves that what we are seeing is just us. We have also been guilty of hammering a person with our interpretation of the Word of God, instead of seeking the counsel of the Lord regarding the matter before approaching someone. The Word tells us when we see (behold) someone who has fallen into sin, then, "…you who are spiritual are to restore this one in the spirit of meekness, considering yourself (taking heed, contemplate, observing), lest we are also tempted." (Gal. 6:1) The next verse instructs us to bear the burdens of others, thus fulfilling the law of Christ. However, if we are inattentive, we can't see another person's heaviness and if we hide ourselves from others, then our brothers and sisters in Christ will seem uncaring.

We have also been boastful and proud in the Body of Christ. However, I believe we are to examine ourselves more carefully by the Word of God, not by our successes, our associations, or the size of our buildings. Remember, that only what's done for Christ, in His manner and in His love will last.

We are worthy, we are favored and are all beloved of the Lord. We are no better than our brother or sister and we are not less. This manner of life is possible in God and it is the way He desires us to walk with one another.

What does this have to do with fortitude? Fellowship! We need each other. All of us are members of one body. Without you I am incomplete and part of my body is missing. No matter how insignificant we may feel, we are necessary to the proper functioning of the body. The toenail, for instance, is made up of dead cells. It isn't often considered, but if we lose one, we immediately know its value. It is useful to protect the toe and can be a beautiful extension of who we are if we give it a pedicure.

I know it may sound a little foolish, but consider, we should be adorned as the Body of Christ in this manner, presenting ourselves as a beautiful bride unto Christ Jesus our Lord. This isn't the outward adorning, but the perfecting of the saints through fellowship. We are built up as a holy temple for our Lord and beloved you are a necessary part of this body. In this way, the Body of Christ is fortified.

Journal Notes

_____
_____
_____
_____
_____
_____

Chapter 6
The Wisdom for Fortitude

Finally, I would like to examine Proverbs Chapter 8, which calls us to consider wisdom as a person. In writing these words, Solomon speaks of wisdom as a woman. Understanding this, our deliberation should begin with Proverbs 31:10–31. This passage presents us the model of a virtuous woman and in order to comprehend the 8th Chapter of Proverbs the image of a virtuous woman should be seen.

Our reflection has been about the Body of Christ, which is also referred to as the Bride of Christ. If we are to discern the aforementioned Scriptures we must know what a virtuous woman is like. I recognize that as a man my understanding regarding the female nature may be limited. However, I believe the verses in Proverbs 31 gives us a clear representation of what womanhood is to be. As I study this, I am reminded we are to behold this passage of Scripture in the Spirit. If our reasoning is in the natural, we will all argue, resist, or question the revelation we are given.

This is noteworthy! It is impossible for a person to accomplish anything of eternal value without beholding the matter in the Spirit and by the Spirit walk it out. If you are born of God, born again by the blood of Jesus Christ, washed in the water of His Word and have confessed Him as your Lord and Saviour, you are part of the precious family of God and you belong to Him. From this position in Christ, as beloved children of God and being the precious Bride of Christ, we will reflect upon these Scriptures.

A virtuous woman is the very definition of the Bride of Christ Jesus, though we often fall short of this. Don't dwell upon this in self–pity or constant accusation. Repentance is granted through Jesus Christ! So, repent and abide in His redemption as one forgiven. Jesus bore all the sins we committed, yes, even the sins we have yet to commit. By His blood, our access to the throne room of grace is assured! And, this glorious work of grace through Christ is how and why we can draw near to God. So, come!

To continue, what is a virtuous woman? Well, let's see how she is described and consider the meaning of the word "virtuous". The Hebrew word used for virtuous is <u>Chayil</u>. This expression has a number of meanings based on the context in which it is used. The definitions are: a person or man of valor, strength, substance, ability, might, efficiency, wealth, force, virtuous, an army.

Is the Body of Christ virtuous? Yes, we have at times exhibited every one of these traits. However, we are to endeavor in the Spirit to portray these characteristics. As we read through Proverbs 31:10–30, we discover a great deal more of what we are to be as the people of God and the Bride of Christ:

➢ She is trustworthy (verse 11). Her husband is not

abased by her or made lower because of her and he will never need to result to ill-gotten gain because he is confident and secure in her actions and his heart is safe with her.

- She bountifully deals with her husband and does him good all her days (verse 12). This verse says she will do her husband good. The word good in the Hebrew is _Towb_. It means good, precious, favor… She favors and enriches her husband and will never do him evil, harm, or bring affliction, hurt or pain to him.

- She is resourceful (verse 13). She seeks diligently to clothe her household and finds wool and thread to make the clothes her family needs.

- She is diligent (verses 14, 15). She searches out and fills her storehouse with food for her family. She continues long hours preparing food for her household and delivers a portion to the young maidens she is charged with overseeing as they attend to her.

- She has vision (verse 16). She beholds a field and sees it will be fruitful and buys the field, then, with the seeds she has gathered, she plants the vineyard.

- She is faithful (verses 17, 19). She sees the work before her, puts on her belt and encourages herself for the task.

- She has understanding (verse 18). She tastes, perceives that what she does and what she holds has great value. Her light continues to shine into the night and isn't extinguished. She works knowing the seasons.
- She is merciful (verse 20). She sees the needs of others and gives to the poor and needy out of her substance.
- She is confident (verse 21). She knows winter is coming, but her household will be warmed with the fine clothes she has provided.
- She is industrious (verses 22, 24). She is skilled in the things she undertakes and all her works are exemplary. She sells her merchandise and prospers by it.
- She has integrity (verse 23). Her husband is known among the elders of the city because of her and he is exalted because of her.
- She is honorable (verse 25). She is clothed with strength and honor (Excellency, an ornament of splendor). Her rejoicing shall soon come.
- She is wise (verse 26). She speaks and her counsel is good and out of her heart comes the instruction of lovingkindness, mercies and goodness.
- She guards her ways (verse 27). She is like a watchman who guards a city. She watches over the ways of her household and doesn't consume away her time being idle.

- ➢ She is blessed (verse 28). Her children are established and proclaim blessings over her. Her husband also blesses and praises (celebrates) her.
- ➢ She excels (verse 29). She is one who excels and is blessed above all.
- ➢ She is praised (verse 30). She is virtuous because she fears (reverences) the Lord and because of this she is praised.

These are just some of the truths that are evident here regarding a virtuous woman. Remember, we are looking at this because Solomon speaks of wisdom as a woman. In other words, the Spirit of Wisdom is likened unto Proverbs 31. This is the nature, the manner of wisdom. It is important that we continue to receive understanding of these passages by the Holy Spirit.

Let's continue to consider the manner of wisdom and what is truly true as the Holy Spirit leads us on toward our goal, obtaining fortitude.

I have been contemplating the many things my Lord has shown me, revisiting them over and over. My desire is that I would not overlook or disregard what He has been revealing to me.

Over the past few months we have seen many changes in our world. There are financial, social and political issues that look to be insurmountable. However, we have been assured by the Word of God of His keeping in the midst of the storms. This is the reason it is extremely essential we continue in His Word and in prayer.

The Holy Spirit has revealed to me a number of things regarding this season and I am more aware than ever that I need my Lord's equipping to be able to stand in these times. There are numerous events yet to come. However, our Lord is making them known and strengthening us unto victory for His Holy Name's sake.

I believe this is one reason He leads us to consider Proverbs Chapter 8. Here again, we are beholding the ways of wisdom. I would like to highlight a few things in Chapter 8, allowing you the joy of searching out the remaining Scriptures for yourselves, finding the delight of hearing the Lord speak to you as He has me.

Proverbs 8:12 (NKJV) reveals to us that wisdom dwells with prudence and finds out knowledge and discretion. So, if wisdom dwells with prudence, what is it? Prudence is an interesting word. The definition according to the *Merriam Webster Dictionary*[5] is: the ability to govern oneself by the use of reason, wise or shrewd in the management of affairs, skill and good judgment in the use of resources, caution or circumspect as to risk or danger. However, there is more to this meaning since the etymology of the word is an alteration of the Latin word <u>*Providentia*</u> or Providence. Providence is defined as; divine guidance or care, God conceived as the power sustaining and guiding human destiny.

Now then, we can surmise by looking at the latter that true wisdom is of a godly nature, whose counsel gives us the ability to exercise our affairs with godly reason, care and judgment.

We observe in verse 12 as well that wisdom seeks true knowledge. She finds out knowledge of wise actions. She desires true

---

[5] Source: Online *Merriam Webster Dictionary*.

knowledge and seeks it out. This is confirmed to us by the next verse which instructs us regarding the fear of the Lord.

The first Chapter of Proverbs speaks to us regarding the fear (reverence) of the Lord as the beginning of knowledge. Here in Chapter 8 it says wisdom seeks knowledge and discretion. The knowledge she seeks is in understanding the fear of the Lord.

When we understand our enemy, we can learn more about who our friend is. The fear of the Lord is to hate or make an enemy of evil. Whatever is an enemy of God, and His decrees, is to be my enemy. I hate what my God hates and love what my God loves. Wisdom declares her reverence for the things which are true and of the truth and her hatred for the things God hates.

Through the fear of the Lord verse 14 is understood. As we seek true knowledge and understanding, through the fear of the Lord our God, we find counsel and sound wisdom to be present. We also obtain, through the counsel of wisdom, understanding and strength. Wisdom is speaking of herself in this verse, but is offering herself to us.

Wisdom manifests her love for us as the children of God and instructs us that if we seek for wisdom we will find her. Her ways are the ways of righteousness and her fruit is better than the things this world offers. Wisdom has ever been with God and her delights are with the children of God. Her cry is ever going out unto God's beloved children to listen. For, "…blessed are they that keep my ways." (Proverbs 8:32) Again, in verse 33, wisdom cries out for us to hear instruction and by hearing be wise and refuse it not.

The reward for hearing is found in verses 34 and 35 of Proverbs Chapter 8. Blessed is the man (male or female) that listens to me, the one who is diligently looking for me in every place and situation. For the one who finds me, finds life and "…shall obtain favour of the Lord."

God's desire is that we have life and that more abundantly and in every generation He has been seeking the lost, the broken and wounded. He loves you and me! We are never hidden from Him. He knows where we are, what we are going through and has provided His beloved Son for our hope and future.

I would encourage each person who reads this to carefully study the book of Proverbs. Throughout the book of Proverbs we hear the call of wisdom to the children of men, the desire of God the Father being proclaimed for life. Wisdom continues calling out to us declaring this truth.

Do we now have fortitude? I submit to you that fortitude is found in the intimacy of faith in Christ Jesus alone. He is the living Word and as He has counseled we behold Him. Yes, we have fortitude as we believe Him, trust Him and rely upon Him to fulfill His Word in us. I find I have no strength in and of myself. There are still troubles and trials we encounter, battles to be fought, wars to be won. Our lives are not complete yet. The final word has not been written about our lives here on earth. However, my hope and assurance is in Christ alone. He is my strong tower, my refuge, my fortress, my sun and shield.

Yes, there are many voices clamoring for our attention in this season of life, but there is only one voice of truth. The word He speaks is spirit and life and He beckons us on in truth.

Through every Scripture considered, we've discovered Jesus lovingly correcting, gently leading and gloriously revealing Himself. He is our loving Shepherd and will never ever leave us. The following is picture of what I have seen in Psalm 23 while meditating upon my loving Shepherd.

The Lord, who is the eternal self-revealing One, the great Creator and perfect loving Father, is my Shepherd. As my perfect Shepherd and Pastor, He keeps, feeds, and nourishes me. He is my closest Companion and Friend, my dearest Comforter and Teacher. I will never know what it is to be without Him. I will never know lack because He is ever with me. I may not always have my own desires, but He will always provide for me what I need and what is good for me. He brings me to fresh green fields and there I rest as He watches over me. He carefully leads me beside the quiet streams where I am refreshed moment by moment. Here in this place my Lord restores my soul. My life and strength are renewed and new wonders I see as I walk with my King. He leads me in upright perfect paths for His own Name's sake. They are memorials of Him and He reveals them to me. Though I walk in places that have the appearance of death I will not dread them, for my Lord is ever with me. He constantly assures me as I follow Him. His rod corrects me when I veer off course and His staff lifts me up when I become entangled in the brush. My Lord prepares a feast for me even in the midst of my enemies and He anoints my head with His oil. His holy oil cleanses my wounds and my vision is cleared again. My cup is always running over as I partake of His goodness. I am abundantly enriched by My Loving Lord. Indeed, His goodness and mercy pursue me every moment and I am assured by my Lord Jesus continually that I will abide in His dwelling place forever.

Journal Notes

_____
_____
_____
_____
_____
_____
_____
_____
_____
_____
_____

Conclusion

What do you need today, at this very moment? I tell you He is here to save, heal and deliver. May the Lord God reveal Himself to you in this hour as you call upon Him.

Do not be discouraged but hope in the Lord. He will yet save you. He will come and His coming is soon. Yes, many have asked, where is the hope of His coming? The question of our Lord's return has been something the world has used to mock and ridicule God's children. However, He will come as He declared and receive His beloved Bride unto Himself and we shall ever be with the Lord. He still waits for the precious fruit of the earth. I am so glad that you will be part of this great gathering of peoples. Though I may not know you personally, my joy is in knowing that we will join together with the hosts of heaven to praise Jesus Christ the Lamb who redeemed us to God by His blood.

It is time now to learn to love as Christ loves, hear as Christ hears, obey as Christ obeys and forgive as Christ forgives. We can't afford our petty differences any longer. We need to walk along side one another encouraging and building up the beloved Body of Christ in our most holy faith.

There are many truths yet to learn as we continue this life of faith with fortitude. However, I would encourage each of you to press on, delving into the Scriptures as we have been directed to do, always beholding the Word of God through the eyes of truth, asking for His divine direction.

The Word of God (*The Holy Bible*) is His Story and the blessed book of hope. I am confident that He will continue to lead you as you seek His face. I pray the Holy Spirit will guide you into His truth and that nothing will hinder you from that which He has purposed for you as His beloved child.

I believe the day is fast approaching, though we know neither the day nor the hour. Many seasons have come and gone and we may see many more pass. However, we are not to forecast His coming for we are told that no man knows when He will return. Yet, we are instructed to be watchful, praying always in the Spirit; for He will come as a thief in the night. There is no room for speculation but we are to keep our lamps filled with oil and the wicks trimmed because, the call will come and those who are ready and watching will join in the marriage supper of the Lamb.

What a glorious day we shall soon see! Let us continue to encourage each other in these truths as we see the day fast approaching, lifting our eyes toward the heavens for our redemption draws near! Even so, come Lord Jesus!

May all who read be given ears to hear, eyes to see and a heart to understand, amen.

www.ingramcontent.com/pod-product-compliance
Lightning Source LLC
LaVergne TN
LVHW051506070426
835507LV00022B/2960